Kids Worship
Volume 1

Compiled by Destiny House Publishing, LLC

VOLUME 1

Kids Worship Volume 1

Copyright ©2015 Compiled by Crystal Jones

Published by Destiny House Publishing, LLC

ISBN- 978-1-936867-13-4

ISBN -1936867133

Unless otherwise stated, all scripture quotations are from the Holy Bible, King James Version. Scripture references that do not have the Bible version noted are the author's paraphrase.

Editing: Cover design and Publication

Layout: Destiny House Publishing, LLC

Artwork:

Printed in the United States of America

For information:

Destiny House Publishing, LLC

www.destinyhousepublishing.com

Email: inquiry@destinyhousepublishing.com

P.O. Box 19774

Detroit, MI 48219

Printed in the United States of America

888-890-9455

ISBN: 1936867133
ISBN-13: 978-1-936867-13-4

DEDICATION

To every little boy and girl all over the world. When life seems unfair or painful or confusing, there is a God who cares. He loves you more than you even understand right now. You matter to God.

I also dedicate this book to those precious little people in Children's Hospitals all over the country and those who are sick all over the world. May this book comfort you and help you through as you hope for healing.

Some purchased copies of this book will be donated to Children's Hospital of Detroit, Children's Hospital of Atlanta, and Children's Hospital of Oakland. A portion of the proceeds from this project will go to children's ministries and Nia Imani Academy

CONTENTS

VOLUME 1

ACKNOWLEDGMENTS

Thank you, Father, Son and Holy Spirit for using our little people to bless others.

Thank you to all the parents that worked to help their young people participate in this project. It wasn't easy. We appreciate all your hard work.

Thanks to Nia Imani School in Hercules, California who help educate our little ones.

CHAPTER 1

THE PRINCESS
BY LAUREN DEAN AGE 3

A princess asked her mom and she asked her dad and she asked her brother so she can go to church.

She went to sleep in her castle. She asked her grand mom for candy.

She asked her Papa if she could go to Atlanta.
She asked her BFF can she play with her games.
She asked her Tia if she could watch the Rudolph the Red-Nosed Reindeer Movie.

She went to bed. The princess loved God and Jesus. She pointed to her Grandma because she loves God. She loves everybody.

Dear God

Dear God, thank you for getting me better.
Thank you Jesus.

I want a cracker and drink for communion.

Thank you God, Jesus.

Good tiger
and good praise, God.

About The Author

Lauren Dean

Age: 3

Grade: Preschool

Hobbies: Gymnastics

Aspirations: A Grown-up

Favorite Movie: Frozen

Favorite Song: Let It Go

Church Membership: Greater Works Family Ministries

VOLUME 1

CHAPTER 2

I AM SPECIAL TO GOD
BY KENNEDY ALLEN AGE 3 1/2

I have two hands

I have two feet

I have two eyes

I am special to God

I know my ABC's

I know my numbers

I know how to write my name

I know how to count to 29

I know how to work the computer

I am special to God

I know how to color in the lines

I know how to play in my room like a big girl

I know how to take care of my mom and dad

I know how to write letters

I know how to get my own yogurt out of the refrigerator

I know how to brush my teeth

I know how to do homework

I know how to go to the bathroom by myself

I am special to God

I know how to put my clothes on by myself

I know how to call people on the phone

I know how to turn on my nightlight

I know how to reach some lights in my house

I am special to God!

I know how to be patient

I know how to feed myself

I know how to help clean the kitchen

I know how to put on my shoes

I know how to play games

I know how to get my toys out of the toy box

I know how to do jumping jacks

I AM NOT A BABY ANYMORE, I'M A BIG GIRL & I AM SPECIAL TO GOD!

Dear God,

You are the best God! You are great! I love you so much. I like it when you go with me everywhere. I really like it when you are with me when I'm sleeping at night. Sometimes I have dreams at night and cry, but you make me feel better. Thank you for taking care of me even though I can't see you.

Thank you God for giving me a new coloring book, reading books, my doll, my me reader, my tablet, my hair bows, and my toy pet dog. Thank you God for giving me a school to go to every day. Thank you God for my big family; My mommy, daddy, sister, my big brother, and my little tiny baby brothers. Thank you God for my parents that take very good care of me. I want to ask you some things... Are you busy? What do you like to eat for a snack? What do you like to eat for lunch? How do you make all these things outside? How old are you? What do you do every day? I still can't hear you talking to me. I think about you all the time even when I'm not praying. Did you really make everything in the world? When can I hear you? Can you hear me when I sing? My favorite song to sing is "You're Amazing." I'm happy that I can celebrate your birthday! Did you like your birthday party? Did you get any presents? Thank you for my family that you gave me, I am very grateful for all of them.

LOVE, KENNEDY

TESTIFY KENNEDY!

God is a Healer!

I know that I can go to God for help. When I was sick, I missed school for three days. I had strep throat. I had to take my medicine two times a day. My medicine tasted like lemon and bubble gum. I prayed and asked God to heal me and HE DID IT! Now I'm praying to ask God to heal my daddy because he has strep throat. God, you are a great healer!

God is my Protector!

I was at school and was playing in the block area. I felt something on my back and then I turned around and it was a boy hitting me with two blocks in his hand. I laughed because he didn't hit me that hard and I was OK. God also keeps me safe when I'm sleeping, when I ride the bus to school, when I'm in the dark, when I'm scared, when I'm driving in the car with my mom and dad.

GOD IS GREAT

God is great!

He is my friend

He tells me that I'm pretty

He tells me that I'm special

He tells me to be grateful

He tells me to be kind to people

He tells me to work hard

He tells me to be patient

He tells me to listen to my parents

God is great!

About The Author

Kennedy Demara Allen

School: Head Start

Age: 3

Grade: Preschool

Hobbies: Painting, Dancing, Singing, Writing, Reading Books, and Playing on the Computer

Favorite Place To Go: School

Favorite Song: "Until I Pass Out" by Uncle Reese

Favorite Book: Pete The Cat-I Love My White Shoes by Eric Litwin

Church Membership: The Love Culture Christian Center

CHAPTER 3

I BELONG TO GOD
BY ELIJAH DEAN AGE 5

I belong to God.

My Dad says, I belong to him.

When you really think about it I belong to both of them.

If God created everything, then we all belong to Him.

You're my Daddy. He's my Daddy.

You are here, but He is everywhere.

Don't worry Daddy.

You belong to God too.

I love God and

Daddy I love you.

Dear God,

I love you.

I hope this day will be a perfect day for all people

Amen.

David and his Dad

One day David and his dad was out in the field with David's seven brothers. God took the sun from the sky and put it on the other side the earth. David and his dad traveled on the other side of the earth to China. The sun was on that side. David had sheep when he went to China with his Dad. When they were in China, they saw a King called Joey. King Joey's son was named Christopher. Christopher had one million toys. He followed directions all day long. God put a great storm in China because David and his dad went there. Then because the storm was so bad, they ran back to the other side of the earth. They ran from China.

-The End-

David and Me

David was with his dad. His dad said, "God, David doesn't have any friends. Can you create someone that is not born yet? A boy. And make him his friend?"

God created Elijah to be in heaven with David
David's dad said "Can David play with him while he is in heaven with you? Then David had friends more than Elijah.
David's dad said, "Can David have even *more* friends?" Elijah wanted to be on earth with David his friend. David agreed that they were best friends ever. And they always loved each other Elijah and David went to the wild side. A boy lion with a red mane and a dark brown body came out. His face was blue and his claws were black and white. And the lion said "GO AWAY". Elijah ran super-fast like Flash and Dash. There was also a cheetah. Elijah ran faster than the Cheetah. David tried to run fast but Elijah was faster. David got eaten by the Lion. Elijah cried and said "NO, my friend is gone. God can you bring him back please? God made David come back and Elijah said "Thank you God. I know you made David come back" God said to Elijah " When you are born and get on earth, You will have more friends and I will make sure that you will do the same things that David did when he was a little boy"
The End.

Cool Jays

A Rap by Elijah Christopher Dean

Ay God , I love you so much

I hope you be so much

But you are the best

I love you so much

You are the best in the City of David

David and Goliath as told by Elijah Dean

David was in the fields with his brothers and their dad said, "Stop! Stop! Somebody is coming. The Philistines are attacking!" Then David's dad sent three older brothers to the fight with King Saul.

Two of the Philistines said, "If we beat your champion we become your slaves, if you beat our champion we become your slaves!"

Then the Philistines said "Oh Goliath!"

Goliath said, "Who will I fight?" All of the Israelites ran into their tents. This went on for forty days.

David's dad told him to go to see his brothers and take them some food. Goliath was like "ooh what is this? Pizza?" Goliath was like "who will I fight today?"

David went to a pond and got five smooth stones and David said "I will!" Then David went into the middle with the big ole giant.

Then Goliath said, "Am I a dog?" Then David said "you're not a dog, don't come at me like a dog." Then Goliath said, "I'm going to beat you, little boy!" David said "I came to fight you with the power of the Lord." Then, David put the five smooth rocks in his sling shot. He pulled back and they went right on the giant's forehead.

The giant fell back and forth, back and forth and fell right in front of David, the little boy.

The Israelites yelled "Yeah, yeah the giant is dead!" The end.

About The Author

Elijah Christopher Dean

Age: 5

Grade: Kindergarten

Hobbies: Playing sports, watching football, soccer, making up songs and stories

Aspiration: Scientist

Favorite Song: It's A Hard Knock Life

Church Membership: Greater Works Family Ministries

CHAPTER 4

GOD IS MY BFF
By RUCKER JOHNSON, JR. "Buddy" AGE 6

GOD IS MY BFF

God is my best BFF in my heart

God is my big DREAM I want to see

God is my LOVE

God is my state and country

God is my Pacific Ocean

God is my SUN

God is my Earth

God died for us

God is my main person

God is the one and only one that can bless us with presents

God is the Best

God is the World

God is never alone

God is in heaven

About The Author

Rucker Johnson, Jr.

Age: 6

Grade: 1

Hobbies: Writing, soccer, basketball, and t-ball

Favorite Subject: Math

Organizations: Wild About Writing Club

Aspirations: Astronaut and Professional Musician

Church Membership: Shiloh Church

VOLUME 1

CHAPTER 5

GOD IS A GENIUS!
By SHILOH KHAI IMAN BRADLEY age 6

God is a genius!

God's brain is always turned on so he can learn.

He never sleeps.

God is my hero.

I am God's hero, too.

I love God because he helps me to learn.

God is nice.

I love God because he is so beautiful.

God is my shepherd.

God died on the cross.

God is a good God because he saves the people.

God is never bad, He is always good.

About The Author

Shiloh Khai Iman Bradley

Program: Nia Imani

Age: 6

Grade: 1

Hobbies: dancing, singing, acting, writing, drawing, and puzzles. She also likes to make designs out of Legos.

Aspirations: Doctor

Favorite Song: I Give Myself Away by William McDowell

Church Membership: Valley of Blessings

CHAPTER 6

LETTER TO MY FAMILY
BY KYLA DEBOES AGE 7

I

know

that

you

are

having a

bad day

but

just

pray

to Him

and

he will

make

it easy.

Jonah tried to run away from God. God told Jonah to go to the city of Nineveh. Jonah was supposed to tell the people of Nineveh that God won't ignore their behavior. Nineveh was a place where the people did not obey God. They were the enemies of Israel, who God had selected as his chosen people.

Jonah tried to hide from God, so he wouldn't have to do the task that God gave him. He paid money to get on a ship that was the opposite way of Nineveh, called Tarshish. The Lord saw where Jonah was hiding and the Lord sent a big storm. The sailors on the ship were afraid, and bowed down to serve their God's. Meanwhile Jonah was at the bottom of the ship sleeping when the storm came. The captain woke Jonah up and said, Wake up and pray to your God, see if he notices us and if he's willing to save us.

The sailors threw dice to see who was responsible for the storm. The dice pointed straight to Jonah. They asked Jonah: Where are you from? What race are you? What caused this storm? Jonah stated that he was a Hebrew, and that he worshiped the Lord who lives in Heaven. He is the one who created the Land and Sea. The sailors became afraid because they knew that Jonah was running away from the Lord God. They asked Jonah why did you do this? What do you want us to do to calm the sea? Jonah replied throw me overboard and the will calm the storm. This storm is all my fault.

The sailors tried very hard to get the ship to a safe place, but it didn't work. The storm got worse. The sailors began to pray to Jonah's God for help. They asked God not to let them die for taking Jonah's life. They didn't want to be responsible for Jonah's death. They told God we know you can do whatever you want. Then, they tossed Jonah over the ship. At that moment the storm stopped. The men were afraid, so they made sacrifices and promises to the Lord.

The Lord sent a big fish to swallow Jonah. Jonah was in the belly of the fish for 3 days and 3 nights.

While in the belly of the big fish, Jonah begin to pray to the Lord. He thanked God for saving him from drowning. Jonah remembered the Lord and decided to do what the Lord asked him to do in the first place. Then the Lord God spoke to the big fish to spit out Jonah on the sea shore. Jonah went to Nineveh and did what God had instructed him to do. When he got to the city he walked around for a day. Jonah then declared that Nineveh would be destroyed in 40 days. The people of Nineveh believed God and decided to fast. When the King heard about this, he decided to get off his throne and fast too. The King announced a new rule: No animals or people were to eat or drink and they both were to wear sackcloth. They were ordered to cry to the Lord God for help and stop making bad decisions. They had hoped that their good behavior would be rewarded so that they can stay alive. God saw Nineveh's good behavior and decided to save them.

Jonah disobeyed God. Sometimes we are just like Jonah. We do things that we are not supposed to do. This story showed me that when you disobey God, it can take you in the opposite direction. Jonah knew what God told him to do, but decided to go the opposite way to Tarshish.

We can't hide from God. Even when you disobey God, he knows how to come and find you. Jonah was on the ship causing a lot of trouble for the sailors. God knew where Jonah was and caused a strong wind to blow. It didn't look like God was there to help at first, but he showed Jonah that he wasn't doing what he was told to do. There was one time when my parents found out I disobeyed them, and I got in big trouble. My punishment helped me obey, just like God helped Jonah.

We are able to worship God when we obey him. Jonah listened to God and helped out the people of Nineveh. When you obey your parents, it's another way of worshiping God.

About The Author

Kyla Michelle Deboes

Age: 7

Grade: 2

Aspirations: Fashion Designer or Doctor

Hobbies: Dancing, singing, and cheering

Ministries: Choir and dance ministry

Favorite Song: Sunday Morning by Mary Mary

Favorite Book: Chicka Chicka Boom Boom

Church Membership: Galilee Missionary Baptist Church

VOLUME 1

CHAPTER 7

GOD IS
BY MAKAYLA KINNARD AGE 8

One of my favorite verses is, "For God so loved the world that He sent His only begotten Son. For all have sinned and come short of the glory of God."

God sent his only son Jesus to die for our sins.

God is my Savior

God is my hero

God is the one who made the world

God is our Father

God is my shield

God is my Rock

I'm a part of God's army!

 TESTIFY MAKAYLA!

My name is Makayla I am eight years old. In my short life so far, I have walked by faith and God has blessed me. Before I was born my mom had a priest and a nun visit and give Eucharist. They put healing oil on me at the hospital! Mom's hard labor and problems didn't stop me!

On August 25, 2006 at 12:36 p.m. my mom's doctor delivered me and rushed me to ICU (Intensive Care Unit).

I was born blue and not breathing. My little lungs were full of the yucky stuff. My mom tells me God sent angels to surround and watch over me! Mommy also told me that God saved me because he loved me so much and that ALL little girls are princesses because God our Father is the King of Kings.

About The Author

Makayla Kinnard

Age: 8

Grade: 3

Fsvorite Song: See You Again by Wiz Kalifa

Favorite Movie: Stomp the Yard

Aspirations: Psychologisst

Church Membership: Valley Bible

VOLUME 1

CHAPTER 8

GOD IS MY ICON
BY HAROLD DEON DOUGLAS III AGE 10

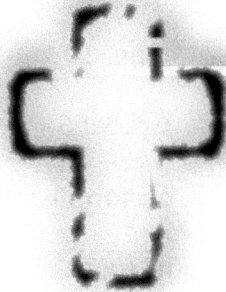

God is my ICON.

I would follow Him until the end of time.

 He gives me guidance and wisdom to succeed.

He tells me which path I should take.

God is my Saviour.

He died for our sins to save us from destruction. He traveled to distant lands.

The priests were jealous of Jesus so they accused Him of treason.

They hung Him on the cross.

But God is filled with happiness.

About The Author

Harold Deon Douglas III

Age: 10

Grade: 6

Hobbies: Drums, football, performing arts, and skateboarding

Aspirations: Professional football player and FBI agent

Favorite Subject: History

Church Membership: Valley of Blessings Church

CHAPTER 9

GOD IS COOL FROM A TO Z
BY JAIMEN ALLEN AGE 10

A- wesome

B-lessing me everyday

C-onfidence that He gives me

D-efinitely helps me

E-veryday He puts food and clothes on my back

F-antastic

G-iving me so many gifts

H-ugs He allows me to get from my mom

I-nside my heart

J-esus is my gift from God

K-ristin and Kennedy (giving me my sisters)

L-oyalty

M-akes miracles happen

N-ice

O-xygen He gives me to live everyday

P-eace

Q-uiet voice that I hear when He speaks to me

R-eigns over all

S-ongs in my heart

T-hankful for Him

U-nderstanding

V-ictorious

W-eather that He made

X-e(**X**)ample He is to all that believes

Y-ours and my friend

Z-ealous

God is cool like the ABC's and He is very loving, forgiving, and important to me! I never want to be without His blessings. I hope that my friends and family will get to know Him better. I want God to be happy with everything that I do. God is so cool. I'm glad that I believe in Him. Do you believe? It's simple like the ABC's.

Dear God,

I thank you for letting me have a family. You have been helpful to my family. When my grandmother and grandfather were in the hospital, you allowed them to get out. I'm thankful for you being there for me when I'm sick. You are with me when I ask for you. Thank you for saving my friend, Jack from a car accident and not letting him die.

When I'm traveling alone, I thank you for protecting me. God, when people die, I wonder if you can allow them to come back into that person's life? I also want to know if you are there with everybody at the same time? Are you there with my family that lives in Mississippi? When I'm alone, I think about what I can do to make sure you stay with me. When I'm sad, I pray for you to help me get through what I'm feeling at the moment. When I'm afraid, I believe in you so I know that you will keep me close to you. Do you ever look around the whole world to see if people are waiting for you? Do you ever get worried about people that are sick in the hospital? How do you know if people are sad? How do you know if people are happy? Thank you God for letting my family be healthy and have a place to live. Not all people have a nice place to live. Thank you for the Seahawks Super Bowl Win. Thank you for a great Christmas! Thank you for everything!

Jaimen's Story to God:

One day I had a rough day at school. I heard that my friend, Jack had got into a bad car accident. Why do bad things happen to people? Jack is a great person. He always listens to his teachers and his parents. He had to have surgery on both of his legs, one of his arms and on his nose. He was in the hospital for a week and couldn't return back to school for the rest of the year. I'm thankful to God that he didn't die. But again, I ask the question, why do bad things happen to good people?

The only bad thing I can think of that has happened to me is when I had to get my tonsils taken out. I was a baby.

I wonder if God will have an answer to my question. I sometimes can hear when God is telling me to do the right thing. When I think about God, I think many things about Him. He is my lifesaver and He is my hero. I never thought that I could know someone so powerful, big, and strong. God made everything in this world and I want to make sure that my life blesses Him. I believe in God, so that means I am a Christian. In order to be a good Christian, you have to believe in God and don't ever say bad things about Him. The Bible teaches me to believe in God even when He is not there and to not get frustrated. I read my Bible every Sunday. Learning about God is so fun and very helpful to my life. I don't know that much about God but I hope to learn more about Him. My dad taught me all about God. He helps me understand things about God.

About The Author

Jaimen Allen's Bio

Age: 10

Grade: 5th

Hobbies: Playing sports, Watching Football, Skateboarding, Gaming, and Doing Activities Outside

Favorite Movie: The Amazing Spiderman

Aspirations: Professional Football Player for Seattle Seahawks

Favorite Place To Go: The Skate Park

Church Membership: Second Baptist Church

VOLUME 1

CHAPTER 10

GOD'S LOVE IS CREATIVE
BY CASSCE BOLAR AGE 10

I love God because he's creative
I love God because he makes patterns and designs.

Unlike the devil who tries to make us stay between the lines.

Looking at the blue skies, I see clouds moving of different kinds.
Reminds me of God watching our every move
Short, tall, little or small
No matter who you are, God loves us all.

Mighty, powerful, protective, moving
These are words that describe God in every single way.

Loving God is not only by saying it or by praying but love comes from the Soul.

My Prayer

Dear God,

I thank you for healing my mom when she was sick, now she's better than ever.

I also want to thank you for healing my brother, even though he's still sick. I know he's going to be alright by your stripes.

Also, thank you God for healing me when I was sick and passed out. I would not be here if it wasn't for you. Thank you Lord for being my protector and provider. In Jesus' name. Amen.

About The Author

Cassce Bolar

Age: 10

Grade: 5

Hobbies: Fashion

Aspirations: Doctor and Hair Stylist

Favorite Movie: Parent Trap

Church Membership: Greater Works Family Ministries

VOLUME 1

CHAPTER 11

WORSHIP
BY JOY LITTLE AGE 10

Worship

Worship is something that is stronger than ever.

That is worship.

Worship is glory that we give to the Lord.

That is worship.

Worship is everything!

We give worship to the Lord, every day.

That is worship.

About The Author

Joy Little

Age: 10

Grade: 5

Favorite Movie: Annie

Aspiration: Veterinarian or Nurse

Hobbies: Drawing and dancing

Church Membership: Greater Works Family Ministries

CHAPTER 12

WHY WE SHOULD WORSHIP
BY ARIELLE JONES AGE 11

We should worship God because God created us
and we shouldn't take that for granted. He also
died on the cross for our sins. If He never died
on the cross for our sins, we wouldn't be able to
repent.

God is our Lord Savior. We shouldn't take
God for granted. He brought us in this world,
He can take us out. He also brought our family
in to this world.

We should be grateful for all the things God has done for us.
We should also thank God for all the lives he has saved in our
family. The lives he has saved in other families are good, too.

TESTIFY Arielle!

I was about 10 years old. I was going into the
5th grade. I really wanted my best friend since I
was little to be in my class. His name was
Kamar.

His mom told my mom that he was coming to my school.
I prayed to God and asked him if he could have Kamar get
put in my class.

I remember a couple days later my mom telling me he
was going to be in my class. I was really
happy . I went to school a week later. When I got
in the classroom I waited and waited then finally
he came. I was really happy.

When I got home that night I thanked God.
I went to sleep that night really happy. I felt
good. It was heartwarming to know that my best friend was
in my class.

3 Tips On Repenting

 When you do something bad you should

always repent after.

 You shouldn't do bad stuff then keep

repenting, just because God forgives you.

 Never be scared to repent. It's a good thing.

3 Tips On HOW to Repent

♦♦♦

First, you get in a quiet room with just you and God.

♦♦♦

Then you get a notebook or journal , pen or pencil or you can pray out loud.

♦♦♦

Last you say a prayer like " God can you please forgive me for my sins I will try not to do it again next time" or you can write it down in your notebook or journal.

YOU ARE EVERYTHING

God, you are everything to me.

You love me.

You care for me.

You gave up your life for me.

You forgive my sins.

You put me in my mother's womb .

I'm cared for again.

You knew my name before I was born

In your mind my life was already formed.

You love me with all your might.

My love for you makes me want to fight.

I'm happy when you're near.

You help me conquer all my fears.

You're with me when I pray .

Your love is here to stay

About The Author

Arielle Joy Jones

Age: 11

Grade: 6

Hobbies: Playing keyboard, Dancing, Singing, Reading Books, and Playing on the Computer

Ministries: Vessels of Praise Dance Team, Jr. Hostess on Hospitality ministry

Favorite Place To Go: Dave & Busters

Favorite Song: Same God by Tye Tribett

Favorite Book: Dork Diaries (series)

Church Membership: Greater Works Family Ministries

CHAPTER 13

MY STORY
BY JEREMIAH WILLIAMS AGE 11

Five years ago I was over my mom house on the weekend and that night I had a dream my granddad house was going to catch on fire. My mom kept saying, "No it's not". So we went over my granddad's house. My great uncle didn't know that there was grease in the stove. My great uncle was going to turn the stove on, so I had to stop him. God gave me a gift. After that most of my dreams come true. I did my best to stop the bad dreams. God gave me a power. I always wished for power and it came true.

If you are good, go to church and pray, you better believe God will do his best. One thing that God wants is for you to pray and love him. And believe in him because God is the King. God gave His son so we can live. Now His love is right there. He wakes us up every morning. God made a huge impact in my life. I am sure he has done it for you as well. He blessed me with two great parents, my mom and my dad.

I thank God even for the small things. When I was 9, I always wanted an Xbox 360 and God blessed me and I got it. When I was 10, I wanted to see a train I saw one 30 minutes later.

I used to be bad and I changed I started praying and God forgave me. If you pray and don't do anything bad again, He will forgive you. God is the best thing to come into your life. God and Jesus come first in my life then my family. Jesus is our Lord and Savior. Jesus blessed my life too. Jesus and God made me what I am now. When I grow up, I want to be a lawyer and a pastor.

About The Author

Jeremiah Williams

Age: 11

Grade: 6

Hobbies: Basketball, Football, Math

Organizations: Junior Coach Play-Works

Aspiration: Judge

Favorite Song: Take Me to the King by Tamela Mann

Church Membership: Greater Works Family Ministries

CHAPTER 14

THE STEPS TO WORSHIP
By TIAJA PERRY AGE 12

There are many ways, and steps on worshipping. People do it and some don't. But what really matters is if your worship is real and towards God.

Step 1

I want to begin with the first step of worshipping, which is to know the meaning of worship. I believe worship is to show treasure and love towards the highest. Without knowing the meaning of worship is like Sherlock Holmes without a mystery.

Matthew 10:32-33-- states that " Whoever acknowledges me before others, I will also acknowledge before my father in Heaven. But whoever disowns me before others, I will disown before my father in Heaven." Meaning that others should tell that you are not worldly and that you are a Christian. But mainly that you are a worshipper of the only one and truly living God. And if you do, then you will be noticed in Heaven. But if you don't then you will not be acknowledged before God. That scripture goes with the next step.

step 2

which is to be able to worship anywhere no matter who is around. This is very key in worshipping. That shows that you love and appreciate God and you don't care about what the other people say about you. For example, if God tells you to worship him in your workplace then you should do it without a doubt. To show God that you are obedient in his commands.

step 3

The third step on worship is to know the key elements in worship. Which is to focus on what Jesus went through for us and putting God at the top of your list. For example, replace social media for God first. Do you think you can do that? Proverbs 3:6 states -- In everything you do put God first and he will direct you and crown your efforts and success. Meaning your two minutes of worship means so much more to him than you can think. So really mean what you're doing and/or saying.

step 4

The fourth step on how to worship is to know why we worship God. In my opinion, I worship because I want to show God that I love and I am thankful for him. Knowing why we worship is one of the main key elements in worshipping. John 4: 22-24 -- states " Your Samaritans worship what you don' t know , we worship what we do know , for salvation is from the Jews. Yet, A time is coming and has now come. When the true worshippers worship the Father in spirit and in truth, for they are the kind of worshipers the Father seeks. God is spirit, and his worshippers must worship him in spirit and in truth.

step 5

The fifth step on how to worship is to know how. There are many ways that you can do that such as: dancing, singing, lifting hands, clapping and etc. For example, when I went to a teens trip to Atlanta with my youth group G-Rock, our leader made us write to God in worship session. In my opinion, it was good. If you keep a journal and really write in it , you can look back at what you wrote to God, also to see how you grew over that time. But everyone is different.

TESTIFY Tiaja!

A few years ago I was 10 years old. I had good grades and good citizenship and everything. I had a 4.0 all year. I was in the fifth grade. During that era I was so rude, conceited, prideful and all that bad stuff behind closed doors. There was this one boy, well we'll call him John. So John wasn't the brightness student in school. John wore the same uniform every day to school. His uniform had stains. He struggled in every subject and was very quiet. My teacher made me tutor him when I got done doing my work, every Monday. I would always tease him and talk about him behind his back to my friends. During fifth grade graduation John didn't receive any awards for the year. All I did was make his problems worse by teasing him. It didn't help the problem. I was also rude that I had made fun of him until he cried. Later on ,we all went our separate ways and it was time for 6th grade.

My grades really went all the way down during sixth grade. My grade point average was a 2.8 at the highest. I felt so stupid , alone and hurt. Then that's when I knew that I deserved it. But I felt so bad for how I treated that poor boy that I wanted to kill myself. Then one Tuesday, at church the pastor was talking about worship. How to do it why and etc. Also what you can get out of it. You don't just sit there and lift your hands no. You can get relief from hate, lying, pain and etc. Then after that we had a worship session. And out of that session I received so much relief.

In conclusion, what I'm trying to say is, that worship is very important and very much needed in everyone's life. It shouldn't be taken for granted or faked out for attention.

.

About The Author

Tiaja Perry

Age: 12

Grade: 7

Hobbies: Dancing, singing, and acting

Aspiration: Lawyer

Favorite Movie: Pitch Perfect

Favorite Song: He Wants It All by Forever Jones

Church Membership: Greater Works Family Ministries

VOLUME 1

CHAPTER 15

NOTHING'S TOO HARD FOR GOD
BY DAVID IVY AGE 14

God to me is someone I can talk to about anything.

He always has time to listen

I also know for a fact that there is absolutely nothing too hard
for him

No problem, no struggle is too big for God to handle

I look around and see that in six days,

He created this whole entire world

That's amazing.

And that's how I know that there is nothing too hard for God.

TESTIFY DAVID!

I was born into a family of drug addiction and unfortunately my biological mom did the best thing she could do at that time and that was to give me up for adoption.

But then there was a lady name Lisa that came for me and took me in as her foster son. At age 4 she adopted me and she became my mom. She could have picked one of the other kids, but she picked me and for that I am truly blessed. From that day to this one it has changed my life forever.

I struggled in school with behavior problems but didn't know how to work through them. My mom finally took me somewhere I could get some help to work through my problems. I even went to a charter school in 1st grade only to learn that my behavior was not accepted in this school. I was talked about from the principal to the staff of the school.

The principal insisted that he did not want a kid like me in his school. I then went to an alternative school. I stayed on the honor roll and was told this is not the place for me and that I should be in a regular school.

My mom was very helpful in staying on top of my education and fought for me to get the best possible education. This is just a brief description of what I went through, but I made it to the 8th grade and graduated from Medgar Evers Performing Arts School and made the honor roll several times throughout my education. I could not have made it through without God and the help of my mom.

Now I am in the 9th grade doing well, still trying to get adjusted because it's a big difference between grammar school and high school, but I like it. I participate in After School Matters and hope to try out for the track team soon.

During the summer my mom found a program for me to participate in called Just The Beginning Middle School Law camp. I started there in the 7th grade and will be continuing this coming summer. I also was blessed to be a part of the Steve Harvey Mentoring Camp in Dallas Texas in 2014 for one whole week. This was really an experience for me and I hope to go again this year. Just a few days ago I was called upon to be a junior counselor for the Steve Harvey Mentoring Camp.

I am so excited to be a part of a great program and look up to men who can stand up for me and keep me going for greater.

I want to be a lawyer someday, so my mom pushes me to do my very best and encourages me to participate in all of the programs she find her in Illinois.

I attend church on the regular, I just recently graduated from children church in 2014 and was the Salutatorian. Since then I sing in the choir, participate in Sunday School and YPWW. I am in a praise dance group called Brothers of Praise and a part of the Youth Department. We perform at our church for special programs as well as outside programs that my mom gets us invited to.

I love God and my family. God is definitely a blessing in my life.

About The Author

David Ivy

Age:14

Grade: 8

Hobbies: singing, cooking reading and dancing

Ministries: Choir, YPWW, Brothers of Praise, Youth Department

Favorite Song: All I Have to Give by Mali Music

Favorite Book: Blood is Thicker by Paul Logan and D M Blackwell

Church Membership: New First Church of God In Christ

CHAPTER 16

FORGIVENESS
BY MICAH BRUMFIELD AGE 17

Scripture: Colossians 3:13 by Micah Brumfield

Question 1: How do we forgive when we don't feel like it?

Answer 1

We forgive by faith, out of obedience. Since forgiveness goes against our nature, we must forgive by faith, whether we feel like it or not. We must trust God to do the work in us that needs to be done so that the forgiveness will be complete. Forgiveness is a hard thing to do especially when someone has hurt you very bad, but if you have enough faith in God and believe that God will step in and fix the situation, then you have nothing to worry about.

Philippians 1:6, "And I am certain that God, who began the good work within you, will continue his work until it's finally finished on the day when Jesus Christ returns."

Question 2: What if the person we need to forgive is not a believer?

Answer 2
Prayer is the best way to break down the wall of forgiveness in your heart.

Question 3: Why must we forgive?

Answer 3
The best reason to forgive is because Jesus commanded us to forgive. We learn from the scripture if we don't forgive, neither will we be forgiven. –

Matthew 6:14-16, "for if ye forgive men when they sin against you, your heavenly father will also forgive you. But, if you do not forgive men their sins, your father will not forgive you of your sins."

We also forgive so that our prayers are not hindered

Mark 11:25, "And when you stand praying if you hold anything against anyone, forgive him, so that your father in heaven may forgive you your sins."

We forgive out of obedience to the Lord. It is a choice that we make.
We receive the reward of our forgiveness... FREEDOM!!

Matthew 18:22, "Jesus answered, I tell you, not seven times but seventy-seven times."

Friendship is...

Scripture: Proverbs 13:20 NIV

Walk with the wise and become wise, for a companion of fools suffers harm.

Notes:

- This speaks of the power of association which helps to shape character
- We have a tendency to become like the people we are associated with. The people that you hang out with get arrested for a crime you will be arrested as well. You are called an ACCOMPLICE to the crime.
- We try to be like everybody else out in the world and all the while God is not pleased but instantly when you get in trouble God is the first person you want to call, you need to get yourself together, step up, and be the man or woman that God has called you to be. STOP trying to live your life like everyone else. Be who God has called you to be. Be a young man or a young woman of integrity. Go with God and let him direct your every path.
- Walk in your true anointing stop running from the blessing that God has in store for you; no matter where you run or where you

hide the Lord will find you one way or another whether you accept it or not. If God said it that settles it.

- Be a wise man and not a foolish one be somebody with power stand up and take your place in the kingdom of God obey the will of God, trust, and believe in his word; stand firm on the word of God and walk in the power of God.

About The Author

Micah Gerrell Brumfield

Age: 17

Grade: 12

Hobbies: Cooking, acting, singing, playing drums

Clubs: President of the African American Male Focus Group, Vice President of the Black Student Union, School Choir

Ministries: Evangelism, Praise & Worship Leader, Public Relations Rep for the Young and Young Adult Ministry, God's Army.

Favorite Place To Go: School

Church Membership: Perfecting the Saints

Other: Micah is able to speak Spanish and was blessed to begin a dual emersion program where he only learned Spanish (until his family moved from the area).

Micah has been in several productions, The Jungle Book," playing Mowgli, starring in the play "13" as Malcom and lastly "Doo-Wop Wed Widing hood."

VOLUME 1

CHAPTER 17

I GIVE
BY AAKIYA ARMSTRONG AGE 17

Before I knew my face or name I was loved
The angels guided me in the way of the Lord wanted me to go.
While I was being led by the angels I freely began to give up all of
me. This is what I prayed to the Lord:

I give you my hands, my feet, my eyes so that you can use them to
do your will.
I give you my heart, my soul, and my mind so that you can cleanse
me and make me new.
For I know that there is no other man on earth that can take away
the hurt that I feel inside.
So Lord I give it all to you, everything that is within me
I give it all to you so that you can have your way with me
I give it all to you
I freely give my all to you, In Jesus name. Amen.
I didn't know until I was of age that I was touched by an angel and
my mind, soul, and heart was protected by God and the angel he
sent to watch and stay with me and in my head to keep the
negativity out.
So now I am learning to live a life where I give everything to God
and let him take control of my life.

WHAT THEY NOT KNOW OF GOD

Hear me, O God! A broken heart is my best part. Use still thy rod, that I may prove therein thy Love. O you have died for me so I can be free; for my sins could have been worse my whole life.

You reached out your hand, God, and showed me the right path. I tried to repent but it was too late and you gave me my punishment. Who more can crave than thou hast done? That gave his only beautiful son, to free us as slaves of the devil, first made of naught with all since bought.

Sin, death and hell, his glorious name quite overcame, yet I rebel and slight the same. But I'll come in before my loss, my father toss, as sure to win under his cross.

Before I knew my face or name I loved. The angels guided me in the way the Lord wanted me to go. I didn't know until I was of age that I was touched by an angel; and that my mind, soul, and heart was protected by God and the angel he sent to watch and stay with me and in my head to keep the negativity out.

The world is charged with the grandeur of God. He will come back and flame out like shining shook foil; It gathers to greatness, why do men then now not wreck his rod?

Generations have tried, tried, and tried, and all is seared with trade; bleared, smeared with toil; and wears man's smudge and shares man's smell: the soil is bare now, nor can foot feel, being shod.

As stretcheth me apart, Lord I do fear thou'st made the world too beautiful in the years I have lived, my soul is all but of me, let fall no burning in my soul. God you have been more than good to me, you have given me more than I can ask or think.

The Lord will make barren your fields and your fairways. My refrigerators will be empty: no steaks, no leg bones, no butter and no cornbread. He will remove my screen doors and block areas where people lie on the bed, undead. For my new "home" is fresh and touched in God's blessing, the lord of heaven, who has no mansion on earth.

Cries are heard from way above and at the threshold and silence reigns in the last place I fought in battle. Holy and mighty in his chamber in the sky, holy the secret of his law he tells his own, holy and all his people praise his mighty deeds, holy he loves the soul, holy is good to those who bare his fear, holy forgiving sin his wrath will not appear.

Lord, pray...pray loud against the noise of the human hand which seeks to drown you out, and appear on quiet soles so that we might understand your footsteps. Exert yourself in order to recognize our prayers even when they appear in a different garment because no prayer ever loses itself from the source of the one praying. Lord take up the speech by which I pray to you. Grant me gestures which have grown within me in your absence, so that I might remain true to my uncontrollable nature and take your weakness upon me.

Lord, you should always wander and never let yourself settle down because there are no longer any dwelling places - only footsteps be loud and penetrating. Lead me all the way to your bread lord so that my world might wake, lord stay with me. When you arrive, we will be light, bread, and water; and the table will be set when the gates open.

About The Author

Aakiya Nheeja Armstrong

Age: 17

Grade: 11

Favorite Subjects: History, English, Math, and Science in that order.

Favorite Animal: Zebra

Hobbies: Writing, watching movies and comedies, designing clothes, reading about world history, dance (hip-hop, ballet, tap, jazz, modern, contemporary, salsa, and belly dance)

Clubs: BSU (Black Student Union), Fashion Club

Ministries: Young Adult Choir, Praise Dance

Church Membership: Solid Rock

CHAPTER 18

GOD, MY HEARTBEAT
BY KRISTIN ALLEN AGE 17

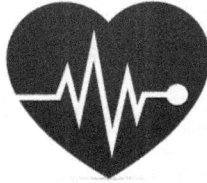

Coming from a background of preachers, the term PK or Preachers Kid never really just fit me. I've tried to live my life day by day up to the standards of a preacher's kid. It never worked out for me, though. The reason is because I've never stood sure in my faith. I say I believe this and I live by that, but my actions never show it.

One thing that I am certain of is God's love. He has never turned his back on me once, and I am so grateful for that! There have been so many things that happened in my life; I just wanted to give up, but he was always there. I may not have felt him, or heard him, but I knew he was there. He's blessed me with many different families that I absolutely adore. He's given me a life that I wouldn't want to give up for anything. I am blessed with two sets of parents and amazing siblings. Knowing that God's love is endless and everlasting gives me such a better way of looking at things. He's not just a random person to walk into your life and then leave.

Once you invite him in, he's there to stay. That is something I really have to wrap around my head. I fall short of reading my Bible and praying from time to time. It slowly became a habit and then a memory. I fight with myself to this day about reading and mediation and it never dawns on me that it's really necessary and needed in my life.

I'm constantly just skimming through the verse of the day or small devotionals. I never just really learn them.

I'm not perfect. No one is. This week I will start a fast with a couple friends. We've decided to cut off all social media for two weeks and focus on reading and learning the Bible. With God's help, I know I'll be able to get through this fast with no issues. He's given me every reason to lean on him. I know that God is always there for me and I have used that as an excuse. Not anymore.

TESTIFY Kristin!

I have no choice but to be thankful and grateful for God. You brought me from being bullied to being able to talk to others about their personal feelings. Thank you. You brought me from wanting to fit in to being able to take the lead and make a name of my own. Thank you.

You helped me realize that people will make mistakes; you can't do anything but forgive them and move on. Thank you.

You pushed me to better when I thought I would give up. Thank you.

After my friends' death, I thought it was the end of the world. I didn't know what was next. I couldn't do anything but ask why. You gave me and my friends' guidance and showed us that it was all according to your plan. Thank you.

Thank you for blessing me with such an amazing surrounding and a reliable place to be able to come and give thanks to you. Thank you for giving me the strength to never change who you created me to be. Thank you for keeping my family together even though we are all living separate. Thank you for keeping my family stable even without a job or a steady income. Thank you for giving my mom such an amazing gift so that she'll be able to spread more love and peace into this world, one woman at a time. Thank you for giving my step parents the ability to love and care for me as their own. It's greatly appreciated. Thank you for my siblings. I know that they can really be a headache, but they are the reasons why I strive to be even better. Thank you for giving me the opportunity every summer to be able to come and worship your name with hundreds of kids that I've never met before.

Thank you for the reassurance of being able to give love where it's needed. Thank you for blessing me with a healthy family, healthy friends, and a healthy body. I want to ask that you heal my two friends, just a quick request, with sickle cell. JaiQuan and Tyreke, they both have the disease and are both in and out of the hospital! Bless them with complete health and much more. Thank you for life in general! Thanks you for everything. "Where feet may fail and fear surrounds me, you've never failed, and you won't start now." - Oceans by Hillsong. This song reminds me that you are ALWAYS with me and that you will NEVER leave my side. "I am yours, and you are mine" Thank you. Thank you. Thank you.

Kristin Allen's Bio

Age: 17

Grade: 11th

Hobbies: Eating and Traveling

Favorite TV Show: Martin

Favorite Movie: Pitch Perfect

Aspirations: Actress

Something Unique About Me: I wear a size 2 shoe in kids

Church Membership: West Point Baptist Church

VOLUME 1

CHAPTER 19

Just For You

The final chapter is for you. Write your own story, poem, personal testimony, rap or essay. Tell of the goodness of God. How has he blessed you? Write about why you love Him. What do you wish others knew about Him? What is something special God did for you? The last two pages are for your own illustrations.

CHAPTER 19

TITLE: _____

BY _____

_____

_____

_____

_____

_____

_____

_____

_____

_____

_____

_____

_____

_____

_____

_____

www.ingramcontent.com/pod-product-compliance
Lightning Source LLC
Chambersburg PA
CBHW071103090426
42737CB00013B/2451